ADVENTURES OF POINT-MAN PALMER

IN VIETNAM

POINT-MAN PALMER

BETSY GRANT

Cartoons and Writings by Vernon Grant

LITTLE CREEK PRESS
AND BOOK DESIGN
Mineral Point, Wisconsin USA

Little Creek Press®
A Division of Kristin Mitchell Design, LLC
5341 Sunny Ridge Road
Mineral Point, Wisconsin 53565

Book Design and Project Coordination: Little Creek Press

Second Edition
February 2019

Printed in Wisconsin, United States of America

For more information or to order books: www.littlecreekpress.com

Library of Congress Control Number: 2014954180

ISBN-10: 098997846X
ISBN-13: 978-0-9899784-6-0

Adventures of Point-Man Palmer in Vietnam is Vernon Grant's story
about U.S. Army life in the 1960s as told through his cartoons with his unique
sense of humor. Grant's biography opens the book. Illustrations include cartoons
drawn for the "Pacific Stars and Stripes" and his OCS Classbook, as well as a
previously unpublished cartoon story about the need for radios for the
foot soldier. The book concludes with selections from *Stand-By One!*
and the complete book of *Point-Man Palmer and His Girlfriend
"Invisible Peppermint" Vietnam.*

Betsy Grant ©bvgrantstudio2014
www.bvgrantstudio.com | Facebook: Bvgrant Studio
email: bvgrantstudio@yahoo.com

TABLE OF CONTENTS

Also published by Little Creek Press:

STAND-BY ONE!

Vernon Grant—Second Edition, October 2015

A collection of single panel cartoons

compiled by Betsy Grant.

TO VERNON

I was blessed to have been loved by this man. I admired and loved him for his modesty, his integrity, his wisdom and his generous and loving heart. He was the best friend I ever had — truly "the wind beneath my wings." I can only hope to give back his many gifts to me by showing you his creativity that flowed from his pen and bringing you his sense of humor that will lift your spirits.

Betsy Grant, September 2014

Acknowledgments

Bhob Stewart was my friend who made sure I made my dream of being published come true. Bhob became a good friend of Vernon in the 1970s when Vernon returned from Japan. I remembered that they would talk comics for hours on end. Bhob was an artist, teacher and writer, wrote *Against the Grain: Mad Artist Wally Wood*, worked for DC comics and Mad magazine, and is credited with coined the phrase "underground comics." He became my mentor and my friend in 2007 after Vernon passed. I only saw him in person once, but we emailed each other or talked on the phone a couple of times a week until his death February 24, 2014. He was the toughest editor I ever had, making his praise all the more sweet. His constant encouragement was critical to the creation of this book. A heartfelt thank you to you, Bhob.

My parents, the late Jean Dyer Reese and Oliver Reese, Jr., created for me a solid foundation of belief in myself with their ever present unconditional love and support for all I did. My sisters, Debbie Kinder and Lisa Hendrickson, have given me frank criticism, valuable editing suggestions, invaluable computer advice and constant love and support. I have many friends who also have supported my efforts and listened to me over the eight years I have been working towards this goal of publishing. My heartfelt thanks goes to Aulga Augelli, Elaine Amella, Sharon Brown Watson, Barbara Bush, Nicole Doctor, Anne Lukaszewicz, Bob and Nancy Miko, Diana Newman, Shushie Pahigian, Barbara Robinson, and Carol Rudder.

I also received considerable professional support that was invaluable to my formation of this book. Cathy Borck, director of Kilbourn Public Library, has given me advice and opportunities to display Vernon's work. Toshiko Cooper, librarian for the Pacific Stars and Stripes newspaper has communicated to other alumni who worked for the paper about Vernon's work. Tony Davis, owner of the Million Year Picnic in Cambridge, MA. (The oldest comic book store in America) has given me much valuable advice, as has also Craig Shaw Gardner, employee of Million Year Picnic and author of the Dragon Circle books and other science fiction, horror and fantasy books. Both were good friends of Vernon. Gary Jones, Chief, Public Affairs at Fort Benning Georgia, has extended me permission to reprint cartoons done by Vernon in his Classbook for an OCS class he attended in 1962. Anne Shuler, owner of Classic Graphx, and old friend of Vernon and I has given much practical advice and expertise. Jenifer Stepp at the Stars and Stripes headquarters in Washington, D.C. gave me permission to use Vernon's cartoons that appeared in the Pacific Stars and Stripes in the late 1960s in Southeast Asia. All of these men and women gave generously of their time to help me, and extended heartfelt support. I truly appreciate their assistance and concern for me and interest in seeing Vernon's work in print once again. ✳

Vietnam Wall Dedication

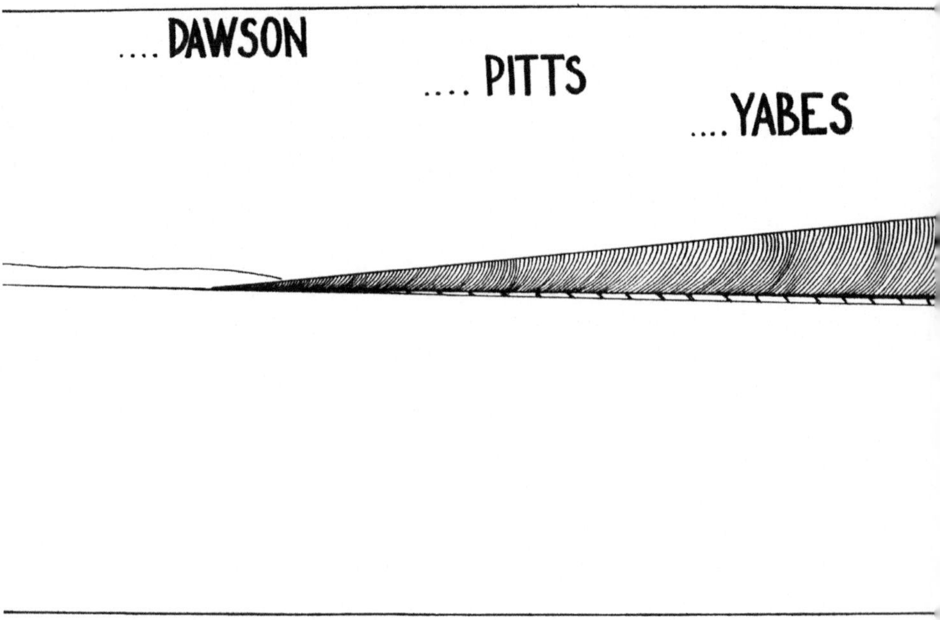

.... DAWSON

.... PITTS

....YABES

Dedicated to four friends of Vernon Grant, who lost their lives in service to the United States of America. Vernon honored them by having his Love Rangers fly by them in this drawing done in 1998.

Pitts, Wilson, Dan Dawson, and Maximo Yabes.

Vernon Grant:
ARTIST AND SOLDIER

1935 TO 1958

THE CARTOONIST

"**J**ust a man who draws funny pictures? No, not quite. His ability to produce these pictures comes from knowledge of Human traits, undertakings, strengths, weaknesses, shortcomings and ambitions. He is essentially a philosopher, psychologist, story teller, historian, chronologer, sentimentalist and realist rolled into one. He quickly sees many sides of issues that escape the notice of the casual observer. A long memory, a quick eye, plus an ear for the unusual are all earmarks of a good cartoonist. Often his graphic accounts of a happenstance offer the comprehensive comment of a transpiring… for a common streak in the cartoonist is the role of the 'self-appointed' critic."
– *Vernon Grant (date unknown)*

I met Vernon E. Grant, creator of two *Point-Man Palmer* graphic novels, *Stand-By One!*, *A Monster is Loose in Tokyo!,* and *The Love Rangers* series at Sophia University in Tokyo in 1972 when he was 37 and I was 22. My journey to Tokyo had started in 1969 with a Judo class at the University of Wisconsin in Madison. Our Japanese instructor and his fellow countrymen in the class, over beer and pizza after the lessons, got me interested in their country. I decided to go to Sophia University for my junior year to experience Japan and to study.

Vernon was graduate student, and I an undergraduate who had only been in Japan for six months at that time. He noticed me first. Always the gentleman, he asked a woman we both knew to introduce us. I thought he was nice, but did not speak to him again for some time. He told me after we became close that he was not only attracted to how I looked but to the way I strode through the lobby of the school with great purpose and confidence. He observed that I took twice weekly karate classes and figured out where to sit in the courtyard so I would have to pass by him on my way to my next class. The strategy worked. I stopped to talk with him and soon learned how much we had in common, even though I came from a white Midwestern (Wisconsin) family and he from a black New England (Massachusetts) family.

Living in Japan I felt very isolated from my family, especially as I was living outside of America for the first time. Telephone calls in that era were expensive. I only talked with my family twice, on the two Christmases I was out of the U.S., from 1971 to 1973. Letters and cassette tapes were our major means of communication. Vernon had been in Japan for seven years by that time. He had also lived abroad for most of his ten years in the Army, from 1958 to 1968, so was much more comfortable living outside of America. He became my best friend as well as a family to me. And I am very grateful that he taught me to become a runner, too, which brought both of us countless hours of enjoyment. We ran every place we ever visited as well as around our home, and we reaped the benefits of good health, increased energy, and enjoyment of nature around us.

It was the beginning of 34 very happy years together, that started in Tokyo and ended in Cambridge, Massachusetts. I write his story in gratitude for our life together, and to show you the art and the sense of humor of a remarkable man.

Vernon was both an artist and a soldier in his lifetime of 71 years. It may seem to be that those professions would be antithetical to each other, but not in Vernon's life. He loved being both.

Vernon Ethelbert Grant was born in Cambridge, Massachusetts on February 14, 1935, to Naomi and Joseph Grant, Sr. Naomi and Joseph had met each other in Cambridge after moving there from their childhood home of Barbados. Naomi worked as a cook. Joseph cut sugar cane in Cuba on his way to America, and in Cambridge was a brick layer, worked in a bread baking company and then sold real estate in his later years. Vernon had a half-brother, William and three other brothers, Joseph Jr., Eugene and Phillip. Vernon was the second youngest son. With William having been in the Army, and Joseph Jr. in the Air Force, Vernon felt inspired to follow in their footsteps. Thus he joined the armed forces at age 23.

Vernon had a lengthy career as an artist. He started drawing when he was three, drawing birthday cards and some early science fiction. Vernon enrolled in one year of classes at a Boston school called Vesper George

School of Art. Vernon's father and an older cousin, Pauline Agard, were both artistic, and urged him to draw. He enjoyed reading science fiction and comic books, with his childhood inspiration coming from Disney comics, Carl Barks (*Donald Duck*), Walter Lantz (*Andy Panda*), *Daredevil, Boy Comics, Little Lulu* and *Archie*. Buck Rogers was his major science fiction influence of this period. Upon reaching adulthood, he learned from studying Vaughn Bode, Robert Crumb, *Tin Tin*, *The Fabulous Furry Freak Brothers* and other underground comics. His eight years in Japan were a cartoonist's dream. The Japanese manga, particularly the Lone Wolf and Cub series done by Goseki Kojima and Kazuo Koike added new dimensions to his artistic style.

Vernon was also an athlete all of his life. He was a Boy Scout and hiked the Charles River in Cambridge, Massachusetts for hours. He played baseball but got more deeply into basketball in high school. He was the Captain of the Intersettlement House All-Star Team of 1951 (when he was 16), that was sponsored by the Phillip Brooks House of Harvard University. He was also the Captain of the Eagles basketball team out of the Cambridge Community Center on Callender Street. This was his first leadership role before becoming an officer in the Army.

I wish I could have seen the Eagles play. They amassed an incredible record of over 100 wins and only four losses. When he told me this I first learned how competitive he could be. To many people who did not know him well, Vernon was a quiet, scholarly man who listened more than spoke. If you knew him well though, and watched him at all the road races we ran between 1977 and 1995, you knew how focused he was on beating as many men as he could in his age category, and racing his fastest—especially at the end of a race. You did not want to be trying to beat Vernon in the final mile, as this was when he would kick it in.

He was a thin youngster when a teenager, and decided to lift weights to change his appearance—as well as become strong. In 1955, he was a two-state Champion (for Massachusetts and Rhode Island) in the 148-pound category for his weight lifting. He was a 165 pound weight lifting Champion at the Cambridge YMCA in 1956 .He also competed in the

Mr. L Street Bodybuilding Contest in 1956, held in South Boston, and tied for fourth place. His personal weight records were lifting 223 pounds in the Clean and Jerk, lifting 192 pounds in the Standing Olympic Press, and lifting 182 pounds in the Two Hand Squats. He was a skinny young man no more.

continued on page 26…

Vernon Grant:
ARTIST AND SOLDIER

**U.S. ARMY
1958 TO 1968**

YOUR BASIC STATEMENT THAT THERE ARE TOO MANY RADIOS
IN THE ROAD DIVISION IS VALID, IF, AS STATED
"RE-SUPPLY AND MAINTENANCE" ARE THE PRIMARY
ISSUES AT STAKE....HOWEVER, THE MAIN REASON
FOR THE DEVELOPMENT OF RADIO CAPABILITIES IN
THE MILITARY IS TO EFFECT EVER IMPROVING
CONTROL OF ALL ELEMENTS. THIS IS THE PREMISE
THAT WE MUST CARRY TO OUR DESIGNERS AND
ENGINEERS IN ORDER TO LOOK FOWARD TO AN
IMPROVED PRODUCT IN THE TOMORROWS TO COME.
LOOKING AT WHAT WE HAVE TODAY AND THINKING
REALISTICALLY, YES...WE DO HAVE TOO MANY.
BUT THE OVERALL CONCEPT OF
COMPLETE ELECTRONIC CONTROL
MUST NOT BE ABANDONED...
ADVANCING TECHNOLOGY WILL
ELIMINATE THE PROBLEMS OF
        TODAY."

VERNON GRANT

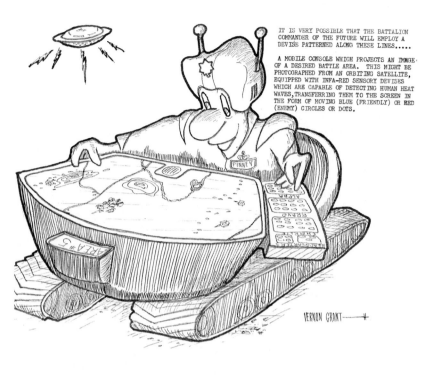

IT IS VERY POSSIBLE THAT THE BATTALION
COMMANDER OF THE FUTURE WILL EMPLOY A
DEVISE PATTERNED ALONG THESE LINES.....

A MOBILE CONSOLE WHICH PROJECTS AN IMAGE
OF A DESIRED BATTLE AREA. THIS MIGHT BE
PHOTOGRAPHED FROM AN ORBITING SATELLITE,
EQUIPPED WITH INFA-RED SENSORY DEVISES
WHICH ARE CAPABLE OF DETECTING HUMAN HEAT
WAVES,TRANSFERRING THEM TO THE SCREEN IN
THE FORM OF MOVING BLUE (FRIENDLY) OR RED
(ENEMY) CIRCLES OR DOTS.

VERNON GRANT——#

HISTORY HAS PROVEN THE VALUE OF
IMMEDIATE RESPONSE TO NEWLY DEVELOPED
FACTORS IN BATTLE. THE AIM SHOULD
BE TOWARD INDIVIDUAL MEANS OF
INFORMATION RECEPTION BY FOOT
SOLDIERS FROM CONTROL ELEMENTS.
RADIO IS THE ONLY PRACTICAL
MEANS AT OUR DISPOSAL.

ARTIST AND SOLDIER

"NATURAL AND MAN—MADE FEATURES WOULD APPEAR IN MINIATURE AS SEEN FROM ABOVE. A CONTROL PANEL WOULD ALLOW INSTANT COMMUNICATIONS WITH KEY PERSONS WITHIN THE PICTURED AREA!"...

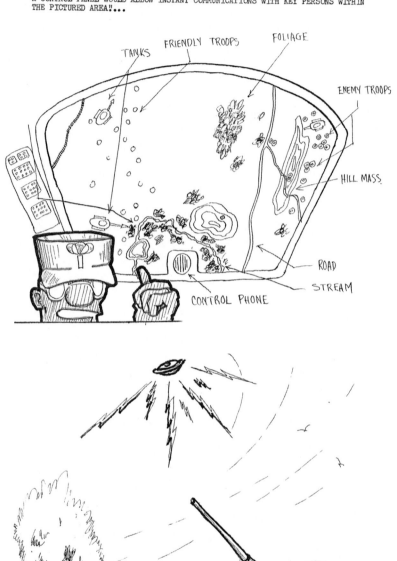

VERNON GRANT

....."SO YOU SEE, GENERAL ADAMS
IN MY CONCEPT THERE WOULD BE A
DRASTIC INCREASE IN THE NUMBER
OF RADIOS IN THE ROAD DIVISION.....
BUT A GREAT CHANGE IN THEIR
DESIGN, USE, AND CAPABLITIES.   IN
THE END I WOULD LOOK FORWARD TO THE
DAY WHEN "TOTAL COMMUNICATION" IS
EFFECTED AND A CENTRAL CONTROL CAN
TALK TO EVERY INDIVIDUAL IN THE UNIT
AT THE SAME TIME!... I PERSONALLY
THINK THE CAPABILITY WILL FAR
OUT-WEIGH THE PLANS NEGATIVE
FEATURES.!!...

3,000+ RADIOS 16,000+

BLAH, BLAH!
RANT'N'RAVE, ETC.

25 May 1964

Dear General Adams,

As a member of the First Battalion Eleventh Infantry at Fort Carson,
Colorado I attended your pre-Swift Strike III briefing at the post baseball
field.

During the briefing you mentioned the excess of radios of an Infantry
ROAD division. In the weeks that followed your statements were fuel for
thought among the communicators of my aquaintance.

As communications officer for my battalion I gave careful study to
your words. While your schedule and primary mission to Fort Carson, then,
did not allow time for a more complete case against the number of radios
in a ROAD division, with "tounge-in-cheek" I have taken your statement at
face value. In my spare time I've worked up an answer not in rebuttal
but in redirection. Your statement was an exciting and provoking to communicators and helped to spur an added effort in creative thought and
efficiency in the use of radios.

Sincerely,

VERNON E. GRANT
1st Lt., Inf.
Chief USA Elm FEN

VERNON GRANT

6 July 1964

1st Lieutenant Vernon E. Grant
Chief, USA Element FEN
1st Battalion, 11th Infantry
Ft Carson, Colorado

Dear Lieutenant Grant:

     I must apologize for being so slow in acknowledging your letter in which you inclosed your carton brochure concerning radios in the ROAD division.

     Please accept my thanks for the brochure which I have looked through several times, and each time with a chuckle. I hope you continue to welcome challenges, for if you do you will find how to win over many of them, and inevitably go a long way up the ladder of success.

     With best regards and good wishes.

Sincerely,

PAUL D. ADAMS
General
Commander in Chief

GENERAL ADAMS: TOUGHEST OF THE TOUGH

THE U.S. officer directing Exercise Delawar, General Paul DeWitt Adams, 57, is reputed to be the roughest, most hard-nosed American commander since General George S. Patton. Subordinates look into his leathery face, freeze before his cold stare and stern lips, dub him "Old Stoneface." The most combat-experienced commander on active duty, Adams expresses his military credo succinctly. Says he: "The man who creates the most violence in a military situation is the one who will win."

Adams has no time to be anything but succinct. Right now he is Commander in Chief of Strike Command (CINCSTRIKE), the unified command that welds Army combat troops and Air Force airlift and fighter planes into a highly mobile quick-assault force. He is Commander in Chief of U.S. forces in an area covering one-third of the earth's land surface, including some 70 nations of the Middle East, Africa south of the Sahara, and Southern Asia (USCINCMEAFSA). In his spare time, he is directing the evaluation of a controversial Army air assault division with which the Army hopes to prove that it needs a large air unit of its own for quick strikes. Air Force officers claim that the Army is merely trying to steal their troop-carrying and air-support ro'e.

"An Open Mind." The selection of Adams to referee this Army-Air Force dispute testifies to his record of cold objectivity and ruthless fairness. Air Force Vice Chief of Staff General William F. McKee recently leaned across a Pentagon barbershop chair to tell Defense Secretary Robert McNamara that Adams was the best man in either service he could possibly have found to run STRIKE. And Air Force Chief of Staff Curtis LeMay calls Adams "the most objective officer I have ever run across in the Army. He has an open mind."

Adams drives himself and his staff to a frazzle. He

GENERAL ADAMS

works ten-hour days seven days a week. At his headquarters on Tampa's Mac-Dill Air Force Base, associates can recall seeing him in civvies only twice: once on a golf course, once in his office on a Sunday morning. He worked his staff on both Christmas and New Year's. One officer was summoned to Adams' office at 4 p.m. on a Sunday, later caught a rare Adams smile. "Have a nice weekend," said Adams. "I'll see you Monday morning."

Genius by Sweat. Even bright junior officers who will not concede that Adams is innately smarter than they admit there is no way to keep up with him. Says one: "If genius is 90% sweat, then he is a genius."

By such sweat, Adams has bui't STRIKE in 2½ years into a 225,000-man force that can speedily deploy eight Army divisions and more than 50 TAC air squadrons to any spot in the world. During the 1962 Cuban missile showdown, Adams alerted some 100,000 men, readied 1,000 aircraft for takeoff, moved some 15,000 armored-division troops to staging areas. Nikita Khrushchev got the message.

Adams developed his toughness the hard way. In World War II, he helped direct the Ranger tactics of the First Special Service Force in the Aleutian Islands and Italy, also served in hot spots from Anzio and Ardennes-Alsace to the Rhineland and central Germany. In the Korean war, he ended up as Eighth Army Commander Maxwell Taylor's chief of staff. He directed U.S. Army and Marine forces in the landings in Lebanon in 1958. Last fall he was the key commander in the huge "Operation Big Lift" that sent 15,377 men and 445 tons of combat equipment to Europe in 63 hours.

The kind of tribute that Paul Adams grudgingly respects is that expressed by one of his STRIKE officers: "I don't like the guy, but if war starts, I don't want anyone else leading me."

19

...continued from page 14

After graduating from Rindge Technical High School in Cambridge, Massachusetts in 1952, he held a number of jobs that included working in the shipping department of the Houghton Mifflin Publishing Company in Cambridge. He told me that in 1958, when he was 23, he volunteered to join the Army to gain secure employment, serve his country and travel the world. I did not meet him until 1972, when he had been out of the Army for five years. He told me then that his ten years in the Army had fulfilled all of those goals.

He began his running career (which lasted until he passed at age 71) at the age of 22, before entering the Army, and knowing he would need that training and endurance to be the best soldier he could be. His running and athletic prowess paid off. When he completed basic training at Fort

VERNON GRANT

Dix in March of 1958, he received the Performance Award Certificate. In a test of strength and stamina, he obtained a score of 361, the highest score in his Company E.

Vernon completed numerous training courses that began with the Basic Army Administration Course, Supply Sergeant's Course and then the Information Specialist Course. Vernon did not stop drawing even while in the midst of serving his country. In 1964, he drew a story to make the point that more radios were needed in the battlefield. His science fiction bent is obvious in this story. It was entitled "Visitation 63 Swift Strike III." He sent it to General Adams, from whom he had taken a course on communications, and the letters they exchanged reveal how Vernon used humor to make his points. General Adams appreciated that as well as Vernon's drawings and story. (General Adams was Commander in Chief of Strike Command, which combines Army combat troops and Air Force airlift and planes into a highly mobile quick assault force.) See pages 16-23.

Vernon was invited to enroll in Infantry Officer Candidate Course in Fort Benning, Georgia in 1960. I was told by an Army officer in 2006 that usually only college graduates were sent for Officer Training back in those years. After being commissioned a second lieutenant in the Infantry in 1960, he returned to Fort Benning three more times. He went two times in 1962, for the Basic Airborne Course and then for the Infantry Officer Communications Course. Finally in 1966, he returned for the Associate Infantry Officer Career Course.

An occurrence of great significance happened on his first trip to Fort Benning in 1960. His journey by train began in Boston. His trip to Atlanta was normal but things changed once the train reached Atlanta. They stopped the train and added an extra car.

Vernon was travelling with papers saying he was travelling to Fort Benning as a candidate to be an officer in the U.S. Army. Vernon was entitled to a parlor car seat travelling out of Atlanta. (This was part of the railroad's contract with the U.S. government, to provide first class seating for officers). The parlor car they had in the train was for Whites only. So they had to add a separate "Colored" parlor car for him. Vernon said he was the only person in the car. However, he did not let this affect him, even when he told me this story.

Once he began the training, he told me that early on he was called to an unofficial meeting. He was surprised to see the meeting consisted of only Black officer candidates. There were ten candidates present. The meeting was led by a Black officer. The officer looked around the room and predicted that only three of the candidates would complete the course. Many of them disagreed, saying they would all be successful. However, the officer was correct. Vernon was not intimidated, and he persevered to become one of the three.

Vernon was the artist for the Classbook for his 50th Company Officer Course in 1962. It was entitled "50th Company OC 1-62." He had continued his art work while he was in the service. In the Classbook there were 129 graduates. Studying the names and pictures of the graduates, it appeared to me that one hundred twenty men were White, six men were Black, two were Latino and one was a Japanese American. Thus, Vernon was one of the 4.6% of the class graduates that were Black. Vernon was an elite soldier to be selected for the OCS course, and he was an elite soldier to graduate from it. See pages 31-44.

I know Vernon treasured his time at Fort Benning. In 1999, he took me on a trip to see it. We spent two nights in a hotel on the grounds for visiting families and we ran all over the grounds so he could show me where he had grown so much as a person and a soldier. He wrote the following story after our stay there in 1999:

Return to Fort Benning, Georgia

Fort Benning seemed unchanged. My first visit was in 1960 to attend the Infantry Officer Candidate Course. I was there in 1962 for the Airborne and Infantry Officer Communications courses. Finally in 1966, I travelled to the installation for the Associate Officer Career Course.

I had changed. I had married. I brought my wife, Betsy, to see my old stomping grounds.

The air was cool and still as we trotted away from our overnight quarters at the Gavin Hall guest facility. Less than a half mile down the road the sharp, pulsive sound of troops in formation caused the hackles on my neck to rise. We crossed the lip of a plateau and came down into full view of the massive airborne activity field. My orientation was heart-stopping and complete. The three 250-foot steel parachute towers still dominated the languid, expansive oval... a field like no other.

The next morning we returned at dawn. The atmosphere was rocked by the electric chants and synchronistic cadence responses of Officer Candidate platoons and elements of soon-to-graduate airborne jump-hardened soldiers.

Betsy and I ran through, around and alongside the disciplined ranks of military men and women and she was thrilled to be formally saluted and called by name at two intervals by sharp-eyed cadre of the Officer Candidate School's headquarters whom we had met the day before. In our run with troops at Fort Benning my wife did not go "AIRBORNE—ALL THE WAY!..." Just far enough to make me proud.

In Vernon's recounting of his Army career, he told me he was treated fairly as a Black man. I only remember him talking of one instance in which an older soldier treated him with disrespect, but Vernon called him on it and the man changed his attitude. He talked all the time of how excellent all of his training was and how much he had learned from it. And he often contrasted the Army with civilian employers, saying if someone did something incorrectly in civilian employment, they often were not corrected, but just fired without explanation. In the Army, one's commanding officer would correct one's actions and teach that soldier to be successful, because that was imperative to accomplish the mission.

In his ten years in the Army his desire to travel the world was answered when he was placed in assignments in Germany, France, Vietnam and Japan. In his off-duty time in France he talked of how he would travel to a local pub in Bar Le Duc and often spend hours there drawing pictures for the children of the owners of the establishment, as well as his own pictures.

Arriving in Japan in early 1964, for the next year he was the Comptroller for the Army at the Far East Network (FEN). As an information officer, he also became involved with the FEN coverage of the Olympics held in Tokyo, and in that capacity met Edwin O. Reischauer, who was the American Ambassador to Japan from 1961 to 1966, and Harvard Professor of Far East Studies. When Vernon returned to Cambridge in 1973, this acquaintance with Professor Reischauer would aid him in working on the book, *Scientific Kanji*.

For the years of 1965 and 1966 he was the Deputy Information Officer as well as Community Relations officer at Camp Zama near Tokyo. At the end of that assignment, he was awarded the Army Commendation Medal for his exceptional performance of those duties. He was also promoted to the rank of Captain in Japan in 1966.

continued on page 45...

For six months the OC bows his will, suppresses his pride, wrestles with his conscience and with iron-like self-discipline, is transformed into an officer of the Army of the United States of America. Yet there is humor and a good way of life in the struggle.

You will find it herein...

ARTIST AND SOLDIER

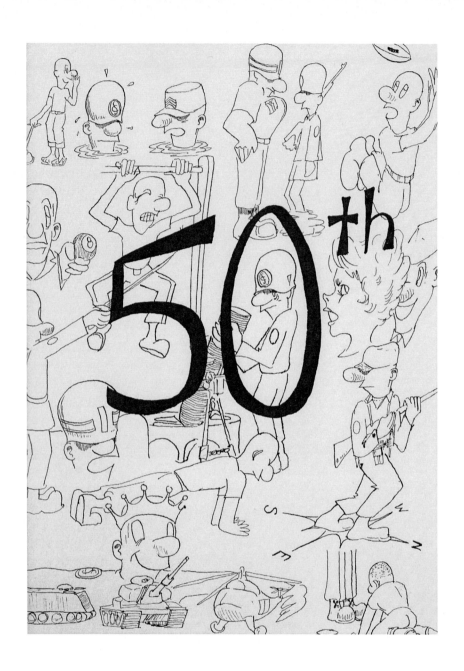

VERNON GRANT

BIVOUAC! It only took 50th 200 meters of march before it shook the "Party-mists" from its eyes, breathed deeply, left its cloud behind, and stepped out briskly for the bivouac area. It was early, quiet, and clean. We heard only the gentle creak of equipment, tough boots hitting the pavement and an occasional cry of warning when the trucks rumbled by. Forty-five minutes later we hit our area. First glance lent impression of only sand, weeds, brush, trees, some sawdust, and washracks but nevertheless, home for a week. We pitched our tents and established order. Then they threw it at us from right and left: patrolling, survival, code of conduct, night and day actions. We tasted soldiering again and shifted to high gear. They drove home time and again that not only is it wise to support your leader, but absolutely necessary. You took over his patrol in a swamp or on a hillside in the pitch blackness. You lead up to the objective only to yield command so that another might lead the attack; hard to take but good for you.

Bivouac was the test and we really hit it "a lick" – convinced them that 50th was a field-functioning company. We felt the pinch on Evasion and Escape. No supper or water before we left. The warning: "don't get captured." If you straggled long enough you found yourself thinking about the thirst, the hunger, and the exhaustion.

You didn't care as much about reaching friendly lines. Suddenly you were sitting on a stump, about two or three in the morning, the moonlight soft on the trees and the OC conscience whispering "I told you so." So you jumped to your feet, took another reading on your compass, and "made it." Some of us were captured; we "grass-drilled," endured the "box," took a bit of knocking about, were interrogated, and then escape... with the dogs looking for you. But we all made it back. That's 50th Company!

2760 opened her doors to her intermediate candidates with a great grin. In we poured and though we scuffed everything in sight, she was happy and so were we. It took a day or two to get squared away. We put some "cosmetics" back on the "old babe"; the floors glistened again and we grabbed our M1's for bayonet training. Odd that we should have been learning how to handle ourselves from a distance of a few feet and from two thousand yards at the same time. The 81mm mortars devoured a week of time and still we did not have complete control. We directed fire in the daylight and the darkness, with and without a fire direction center, with illumination and HE, and when the committee was satisfied, we met the 4.2's (the heavies) and went through it all over again.

VERNON GRANT

VERNON GRANT

VERNON E. GRANT
Cambridge, Massachusetts

"I thought the E&E course was
a 24 hour problem..."

Classbook Staff, 11th Wk. Party

CLASSBOOK

You figure 'em out: Dorroh (Ads), Klump (Money), Goss (Ads), Davis (Photo), Deryck (Photo),
Fedric (Asst. Ed.), Grant (Art), Mills (Layout), Abrahams (Ed.).

The Fifth Platoon is deserted already. Everyone gone. Wonder if I have everything? Display boots, shaving kit; footlocker empty; the candy bar I had taped under the wall locker is nestled in my pocket. Think I'll take one last look around. Watkin's old room — I can still picture him spilling coffee on his display T-shirts that early early AM and then crawling disgustedly back into bed. Hmmm, Zagner's old room — I never did learn what that German floor wax was. Zag was pretty smart all right, heh, heh, chocolate chip cookies for the boys just before Buddy Reports... Sergeant "Queen of Battle" Wilson and Winter bunked here. "Queenie" sure took a beating from Watermelon Wilcut on that Airborne Demonstration Unit he had. And you can still see Winter springing to his feet in every class with the oft-quoted "Sir, Candidate Winter, I have a question..." The utility closet; Grant's "Book-of-the-Night" Club and the location of "George S. Patton" Stiles' delivery of Buffer DD Classes. The latrine — "Our Latrine" — domicile of perpetual gigs; Stone's cockroach laid out therein, gracing a three-inch coffin and Tarr squatting in the corner, shining boots with Kiwi-stained fingers 'till the wee hours of the morning. Across the hall lived Wallenborn and Sundstrom, the latrine's faithful guardians and bright lights on the football team; Wally the rough-house halfback and Sundstrom a glue-fingered end. They had to be good with Lt. Klim glaring at them from the sidelines.

VERNON GRANT

Congratulations to the new officers of the 50th Company. It has been a pleasure serving your class. We wish you success in your new career in the Army.

Compliments of

CHICKASAW CLUB

1219½ Broadway

COLUMBUS, GA.

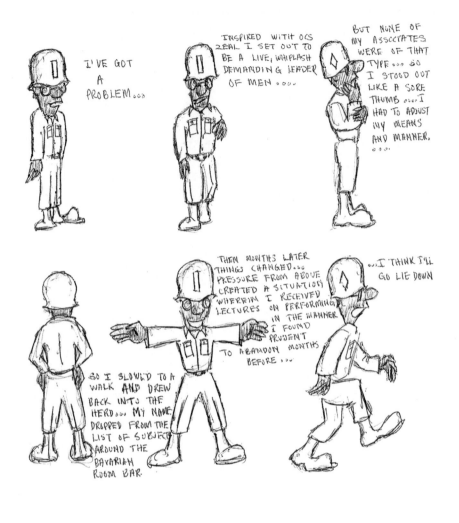

I'VE GOT A PROBLEM...

INSPIRED WITH OCS ZEAL I SET OUT TO BE A LIVE, WHIPLASH DEMANDING LEADER OF MEN....

BUT NONE OF MY ASSOCIATES WERE OF THAT TYPE... SO I STOOD OUT LIKE A SORE THUMB....I HAD TO ADJUST MY MEANS AND MANNER, ...

THEN MONTHS LATER THINGS CHANGED... PRESSURE FROM ABOVE CREATED A SITUATION WHEREIN I RECEIVED LECTURES ON PERFORMING IN THE MANNER I FOUND PRUDENT TO ABANDON MONTHS BEFORE...

...I THINK I'LL GO LIE DOWN

SO I SLOW'D TO A WALK AND DREW BACK INTO THE HERD... MY NAME DROPPED FROM THE LIST OF SUBJECT AROUND THE BAVARIAN ROOM BAR.

VERNON GRANT

...continued from page 30

He enjoyed his duties as well as his time off duty, learning about Japan and studying the arts and the manga surrounding him. Between the years of 1966 and 1969, he continued his cartooning work by doing cartoons for the Pacific Stars and Stripes, the military newspaper for the United States Armed Forces. He would do a page of cartoons under the following titles, "A Grant Time in Japan," "Grant's Heroes" and "Grant's Grunts."

continued on page 49...

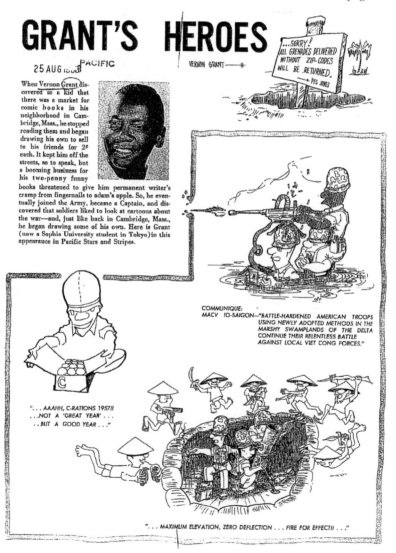

"... Let's burn our draft cards tonight!" ...

"... Yes ... the film is expensive ...
but my enlargment costs have
dropped 100 per cent!"

TAKE FIVE

Readers Look at the Light Side

THE CARTOONS on this page are the work of Capt. Vernon Grant of the Information Office, U.S. Forces Japan. Fledgling (or advanced) cartoonists among our readers are reminded that we would like to share your best gags with all our readers. Address contributions to Feature Editor, Pacific Stars and Stripes APO U.S. Forces 96503.

"Go easy, Muldoon ... it looks like
some sort of trap!" ...

BY VERNON GRANT

VERNON GRANT
©1969

"... Like wow, sarge ... I've had the civilian bit! Yesterday the pool room burned down ... my un-employment checks ran out ... my wheels threw a rod ... the ol'man cut my allowance ... the malt shop closed for the winter, and my chick made the scene with a swabbie! ... . where do I sign? ..."

"... Back at Fort Gordon our first rule wuz, 'never Over load yer belt!'..."

"... 'uess who works in the mess hall? ..."

Sunday Crossword Puzzle
Copr. '68 Gen'l Features Corp.

By H. L. Bisteen

ACROSS
1 Fenny tracts.
5 Polisher.
10 Vegetable for short.
14 Obligations.
19 And others; Abbr.
20 Sphere of conflict.
21 Paintings.
22 Cove.
23 Timid soul: 2 words.
26 See 23 across.
27 Rum ___.
28 Umbrella parts.
29 Tester or trundle.
31 Bristle.
33 Electric ___.
33 City in C Illinois.
34 Immunizing agent.
36 Stripling.
37 Kind.
39 Setback.
41 Authority.
43 "Exodus" author.
44 Surfeits.
45 Varnish.
47 Of a social division.
50 ___ Fail (Irish coronation stone).
51 Ancestors.
52 Appraises.
54 Agreeable.

55 Soap.
57 Muffin.
58 ___ Fixture.
60 Request.
61 Chemical suffix.
62 Pernicious.
63 Avid.
65 Business abbr.
66 Engage in the pursuit of pleasure: 4 words.
73 Desert.
74 TV movie.
75 Wicket sides; Cricket.
76 Lake Balkhash tributary.
77 Sloping passage.
79 Patriotic group.
80 Inquire.
81 Rescuer.
86 Vessel.
88 American inventor.
90 Face with stone.
91 Man's name.
92 Cargo vessel.
94 Resell ___.
95 Persian allies.
96 Greek letters.
97 ___ pitchers.
99 Asian.
101 Fodder plant.
102 Greek letter.
106 Onetime actor Ladd.
107 Thunder sound.

108 Military command.
110 Ike's old command.
111 Tree with white flowers.
112 Boxing champion of 1935.
115 Negative particle.
117 Spring bloom: 2 words.
121 Italian family.
122 Lights.
123 Harmonize.
124 Abounding in ahodes.
125 Active guy.
126 Be abrasive.
127 Bridge mishaps.

DOWN
1 Defeat.
2 Roman emperor.
3 Showy flowers.
4 Lollch specialties.
5 Comes to life.
6 Garden flower.
7 Enclosure.
8 Carves.
9 Gulches.
10 Catcalls.
11 Trouble.
12 Church land.
13 Garden flowers.
14 Faint.
15 Biblical oldster.

16 Showy flower; 2 words.
17 Seed case.
18 Place.
24 Historic river.
25 Building beam.
30 Underworld (Egypt. myth.)
33 Nero or Sellers.
34 ___ of learning.
35 Pianist Hess.
37 Abyss.
38 Assam silkworm.
39 Thin.
40 Bridge thrill.
42 Blockhead; Sl.
44 Muscled.
46 ___ chest.
48 Concerning.
49 Moisten.
51 Man from Monterrey.
52 "One forever;" 2 words.
53 Utah lily.
56 Palm fiber.
57 Interstice.
59 Dwells.
62 Man's nickname.
63 W German river.
64 Lease again.
66 Fevermore.
67 Florida city.
68 Garden flowers.
2 words.
69 Coal mine car.

70 American Indian.
71 Primary supply item.
72 Bakery product.
78 Thrust.
80 Italian wine center.
81 Fortification.
82 Uniform.
83 Shrub with yellow flowers.
84 Valiant Viking.
85 Precipitous.
87 Dogs and cats.
89 Biblical book.
90 Fee.
93 Hold sway.
95 Softening.
96 Popular food.
98 Preserved in a certain way.
100 Half hoop.
101 Part of speech.
102 ___ letter.
103 Guild.
105 Body part.
107 Analyze.
109 Civil wrong: Law.
111 ___ tables.
112 Hypocrisy.
113 Funy pig.
114 "___ Death."
116 Napoleonic marshal.
118 Was corrosive.
119 Part of India.

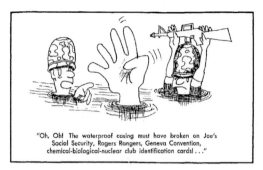

"Oh, Oh! The waterproof casing must have broken on Joe's Social Security, Rogers Rangers, Geneva Convention, chemical-biological-nuclear club identification cards!..."

GRANT'S GRUNTS
BY VERNON GRANT

"If you don't mind coming down, Colonel... I'll give you my ten-minute thing on 'Command Modesty!'...."

"Thanks for the light, Fred..."

"Alright you in the tank, come out with your hands up!"

"Say, Ed!... What has teeth, is twenty feet long, and has skin like a woman's handbag...??"

...continued from page 45

When he was in Vietnam in 1967, he was the Commanding Officer of the Signal Security Force, commanding 400 men at 23 communications sites scattered the length of Vietnam. He told me that he had helicopters at his beck and call to discharge his duties of checking those sites. Vernon did not tell me many stories of his time in Vietnam, but he did recount one time going to a site and seeing a soldier on duty who was high on some drug. He immediately had him removed, and was called on later to testify about the situation in a military court case against the soldier.

He was stationed in Saigon and while there he told me he continued to run. It must have been a dangerous post, because he told me he would have his driver drive along side of him while he ran.

Vernon and I went to Washington, D.C. in 1998. We visited the Vietnam Wall together, and I could see how much it affected Vernon, remembering his time there and his friends he lost. He made a rubbing of four men's names. I think it comforted him to see them together again, and being honored with all the other fallen soldiers. He never spoke extensively of much of his time in Vietnam, but spoke the most of Maximo Yabes, the great Mexican American hero who won the Congressional Medal of Honor for his actions in battle in February of 1967 in which he died saving others around him. Since Vernon has passed, I found pictures of Maximo as a soldier in Fort Carson, Colorado, where Vernon was also stationed in 1962 and part of 1963. I also found a cartoon (see page 50) he drew that he pokes fun at Yabes, so I am sure they were good friends. After the trip, Vernon drew the picture of the Wall (on pages 8 and 9) to commemorate and honor his friends.

continued on page 52...

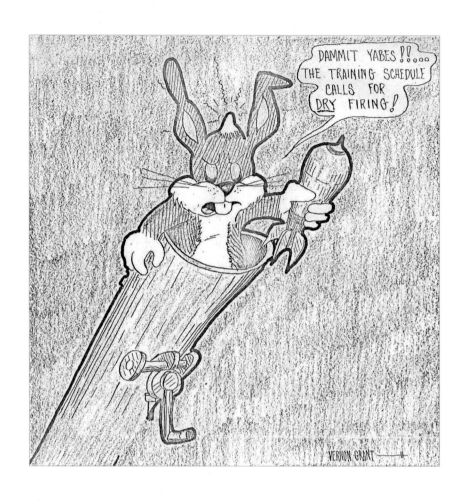

Vernon Grant:
ARTIST AND SOLDIER

**SOPHIA UNIVERSITY IN TOKYO
1968 TO 1973**

…continued from page 49

Vernon's year in Vietnam was the final year of his 10 years in the Army. Right after he mustered out of service in Tokyo, he enrolled in classes at Sophia University, a Jesuit college in the Yotsuya area of Tokyo. A prestigious university, Sophia consists of a National Division with courses taught in Japanese and an International Division that conducts classes in English. He had completed his undergraduate degree in Asian Studies and moved into graduate courses by the time I met him in 1972.

After completing his ten years with the Army in early 1968, he produced three books about Army life and one about Japan. He self-published all of them, and the Pacific Stars and Stripes assisted him by shipping his books to the soldiers in the different parts of Southeast Asia at the same time they sent their newspapers to the military bases throughout Southeast Asia. In 1969, he started with two books entitled *Point-Man Palmer and his Invisible Girlfriend, Peppermint.* One was set in Vietnam and the other in Tokyo, when Private Peter Palmer goes on R&R there. Peter Palmer is a short, bespectacled private easy for young servicemen to identify with.

Peter Palmer's story starts when, at the age of 19, he volunteers for military service and to go to Vietnam. He kisses his shy, flat-chested girlfriend, Paula Peppermint, goodbye. She returns to her bedroom, and "displaying the form that gained her a 'D' in chemistry hastily mixes a batch of special fluid found in an old USAFI textbook." She then drinks the mix, and is transformed into the new Peppermint, who is mini-skirted, with 40-22-36 dimensions—a young man's dream. Even better, she can become invisible, which makes it possible for her to accompany Peter Palmer to Vietnam, and Tokyo. (In the graphic novels, sometimes we see her, and sometimes we don't.) Palmer, due to a snafu is mistakenly sent to a Marine camp instead of Fort Dix and given all sorts of specialized training (Ranger School, The War College, Parachute Training, the Command and General Staff School, etc.). The Army discovers the mistake and then sends him back to basic training for the Army. Vernon packs every panel of this private's story with jokes. On his flight to Vietnam, a soldier wears a very tall helmet with a sign on it saying "Do Not Fill Past This

Line." He is waited on by a buxom black stewardess who asks, "Can I get you anything? Coffee, tea, a headshrinker?" In the next panel, another attractive stewardess walks by with a book entitled *"Dracula on R&R."*

Vernon's extensive experience with the necessity for secrecy, and working in communications, heavily influenced this story. Private Palmer immediately gets in trouble in Saigon by revealing military secrets to a woman in a bar. We see two Vietcong crouched under his table with a tape recorder with the label "Zony" on it. They escape with the tape. Peter Palmer is picked to be the Point-Man due to his expertise gained with the Marines. Peppermint is ever present to help him, catching a grenade thrown at him and tossing it back to the enemy. When Palmer is parachuted into enemy territory to retrieve the tape and goes to a local bar, we see more corny jokes, like a sign posted saying, "No credit to anyone wearing a green beret" and a sign on the road beside it entitled "Ho-We-Win Trail." Book one ends with the Viet Cong torturing Palmer by force-feeding him nuoc-mam (fermented fish sauce). Peppermint goes into a nearby swamp and arms herself with fish.

Book Two begins with Peppermint defeating the Vietcong by force-feeding them those fish from the swamp. She then unties Palmer, and together they bring the enemy and tape back to Saigon. Although Palmer has only been in country for two days, he is mistakenly loaded onto a plane taking soldiers to Tokyo for R&R. Peppermint goes along. Vernon continues his method of entertaining, as well as training soldiers how to act in foreign countries, by showing a briefing given to the soldiers starting their R&R. A Black officer (one of many Black officers and soldiers in his books) says in his briefing, "And while you're here in Japan, don't whistle, wink, hustle, bother, trouble, bite, solicit, pinch, condemn, chew-out, heckle, vilify, denigrate, swear at, embarrass, ridicule, bump, intoxicate, make-fun-of, or laugh-at any of the girls!" Palmer asks, "Can we breathe on them?"

Palmer has many adventures including subway rides and drinking sake. He thoroughly enjoys the experience of having a beautiful woman treat him to a Turkish bath and massage. He then learns about sushi, has a lesson at a local martial arts studio and ends the evening at a local bar.

This starts as an embarrassing experience being asked to dance on stage. But the derision at his tentative steps gets him mad, and he cuts up with some incredible dance steps to applause from all watching. Both books are full of military and local humor and beautiful buxom women and give a hilarious slice of Army life in the Vietnam era.

Vernon's next project was *Stand-by One!* a cartoon book of single-panel humor about Vietnam. One picture shows a subway station in the jungle called "Hanoi Express" which refers to the North Vietnamese infiltration. The cover shows a Vietnamese farmer in a rice paddy trying to appease a large Black soldier pointing a gun at him by holding a sign saying "Soul Brother." In an interview with the *Cambridge Chronicle* newspaper in 1977, Vernon revealed that "I (Grant) became an institution for the U.S. G I's who sought comic relief from the danger of combat and the boredom of army life. More soldiers read (my books) than any other cartoonist or writer in the front. I still get embarrassed when I meet someone on the street who recognizes me," he says bashfully. Vernon went on to say that *Stand-by One!* sold out of all of its 13,000 copies.

After these Army books, shortly before he met me at Sophia University, he produced **A Monster is Loose in Tokyo**, published by the Charles Tuttle Publishing Company, in 1972. Vernon had become deeply involved in reading Japanese comics and knew the great interest the Japanese had in monsters. Vernon thought there were some 350 monsters portrayed in comic books in Japan in 1977. In that same *Cambridge Chronicle* article Vernon said "The television stations have monster funerals when they have to kill off a favorite."

In an article done by the *Pacific Stars and Stripes* in 1972, Vernon said, "Translating life into humor is the biggest thing with me." He added, "Japanese illustrators are the greatest action artists I have ever seen. In my *Monster* book I try to apply composition angles unused by American cartoonists… angles I learned here in Japan." The interviewer lauds "Grant's tongue in cheek tongue-lashing of our human foibles" in the book.

Vernon's own monster is a quirky looking eight-foot tall creature with two ears that cock at different angles depending on his mood; a big belly, long fingers, big padded feet and a tail extending out some 15 feet that he uses as a weapon, as well as way to move the people around him. Extending out from his snout are two differently shaped fangs. But what really caught my attention about his Monster was his face. This was the first art I had seen by Vernon that seemed to be a self-portrait. When the Monster is scheming his next action, his forehead wrinkles like Vernon's. And the eyes often show the same mischievousness I saw in him.

The Monster is in control from the moment he steps off the airplane in Tokyo. When going through Customs, the police are immediately suspicious of this strange "foreigner" with no passport or luggage, and they suspect he is carrying gold bars under his "costume." They start chasing him through the airport, and the chase continues throughout the whole book. He goes on the subway where he sees three young mothers letting their children sit on the seats of the crowded car while they stand up. The Monster takes his tail, scoops up all of the children, flips them up in the overhead shelves over the seats and plops himself down.

He runs into a student demonstration (very common in those times in Tokyo) and frightens one of the student leaders, whom he tells to go home, because his TV was "getting cold." He runs into a Turkish steam bath, and we are afforded a good look at what happens inside. There are humorous vignettes such as when he goes into a restaurant and a fawning pet owner puts her little dog on the counter to eat a cheeseburger. Our Monsters' appearance frightens the owner into leaving the restaurant, to the relief of the other patrons sitting nearby. One page clearly shows Vernon's experiences when he pictures five white birds sitting on a telephone line keeping themselves far away from one black bird perched off by himself, three feet away. The white birds glare at the solitary bird. The Monster jumps up next to the black bird and pulls him close—and the white birds are chagrined. It is a strong commentary on this and all cultures. The book is full of stories of Japanese life, and foreigners' experiences therein, as represented by the Monster.

I met Vernon, I believe, soon after *A Monster is Loose in Tokyo!* was first published. He was a modest man and did not speak much about it, focusing on our relationship and our lives together. However, I do remember he would often take me into the Kinokunia bookstore in the Ginza section of Tokyo to see the book on display, and check on its placement on the shelves. He was very proud of the book.

People have asked me how it felt to be a racially mixed couple in Japan. I first had to learn to adjust to being a *gaijin* which means "outsider." When I lived in Japan in the early 1970s, it seemed that anyone who was not racially Japanese was a *gaijin*.

This was not an issue when I was with my Japanese friends I had first met at the University of Wisconsin in Madison who treated me as an individual. However, when I was on the trains or walking around the city I often heard Japanese people exclaiming *gaijin (short for gaikokujin, someone from "outside" of Japan) as* I approached. I even remember seeing a young mother and father point me out to their toddler, teaching him I was a *gaijin*. It was my first time to have an awareness of what it meant to be identified by race. Therefore, when I was with Vernon, we were on the same footing, both foreigners. He helped me learn to adjust to being under the microscope out in public, being seen primarily as a *gaijin,* and to accept it as part of my life in this new place. Amongst the students at Sophia University, there were white, black and Asian students from America, Japan, and Europe and all over the world, as well as many mixed couples. It was a very comfortable place to be.

Besides working many hours at the drawing board, Vernon spent a lot of time traveling around Tokyo. The classes at Sophia University were ideal for both of us. We were both night people, and the courses we attended in the International Division were all held between five and ten p.m., as the National Division held day classes in our classrooms. Therefore, we could get up late, do our studying in the morning and spend the afternoon visiting places or people. Vernon went to many coffee houses for comic book fans and met both artists and fans there.

Before I met him, he always had a very active social life. In fact, I felt very fortunate that some other woman had not scooped him up before we met and got married. Before we met in 1972, he had a Japanese girlfriend. As he said to Jason Thompson in a *Pulp Magazine* interview (May 12, 2001 "I was going with a Japanese girl over there at the time whose father was the third highest-ranking person at one of the major ministries, and she had use of his card, his meshi, which allowed us to travel around. I would guess I've been in some places that maybe foreigners would never get to see in a lifetime."

I remember two trips we took together that added to my enjoyment of Japan. We took a train to Nikko, a popular spot to enjoy the beauty of the mountains and woods of Japan. This was an elixir for me, to get out of the huge metropolis of Tokyo and revel in being in an area similar to the Wisconsin countryside. I also highly enjoyed our trip to Kamakura, near the ocean. We took a special long distance train that has cars that were called "Romance" cars. They were very plush with high backed seats for more privacy. I especially remember enjoying ordering some tea to which Vernon added whisky.

Kamakura is known for the giant Buddha which soars 43 feet into the air. One can walk up the steps inside of it and look out of the eyes of the Buddha. It was built in 1252, and is the second largest Buddha in Japan, weighing around 93 tons. Another highlight of the trip was eating a delicious dinner at a German restaurant called Sea Lion. Vernon knew all the best restaurants, not only there but throughout Tokyo.

Vernon was one of the most modest men I have ever met in my life. He would talk enthusiastically for hours about causes he believed in or things that interested him. But when it came to what he had accomplished, I often had to drag things out of him. I think this was because his mother was the same, although I never knew her, as she had passed away in 1969.

He had a strong and positive sense of his own identity. He did not need others to give him self worth. He also kept quiet on many of his accomplishments because he told me many people are suspicious of others' successes, and believe others are making up things. So I was surprised when he ventured once that he felt at times like the "King" of Tokyo. He did have good reason to feel so. He had done artwork for the Pacific Stars and Stripes from 1966 through 1969. While a student at Sophia, he drew cartoons and did book and movie reviews for the Mainichi Daily News, one of only two English newspapers in Japan.

In late 1972, Vernon also wrote a singular three-part series about *The Lone Wolf and Cub (Kozure Okami)* written by Kazuo Koike and illustrated by Goseki Kojima. He published the series in the *Mainichi Daily News*, and it was later reprinted in *The Comics Journal* in issue #94 in October 1984. Vernon had chanced upon the story, reading it in a weekly magazine called *Manga Action*. He was fascinated with it from its first appearance in 1970. The story quickly became a national favorite with men and women alike. Vernon had a great interest in studying *kanji* (Chinese characters that are used in the written Japanese).His artistic talent helped him more easily learn, interpret and write *kanji*. This ability contributed to helping him read *The Lone Wolf and Cub* in Japanese and have an understanding of the series. His series was the first in depth study done by a Westerner of this story.

continued on page 60…

Vernon Grant:
ARTIST AND SOLDIER

...continued from page 58

I completed my bachelor's degree in History from Sophia University in 1973, and we both returned to the United States and began a life together in Cambridge, Vernon's home town. He immediately became involved in many new avenues of work. He worked part-time as a taxi driver and drew a comic story (never published) called *"Harry the Harvard Freshman."* Soon after we were married in 1978, we moved into an apartment in a large house owned by Dorothy Williams. She lived downstairs, and she generously provided day care for her numerous grandchildren. Vernon loved children, and would visit with them between his art and work. He became like a grandfather to them, urging them to study and draw. When they discovered he was an artist, they beseeched him for a picture. He would readily comply, but soon began saying he would draw for them only after they produced a picture for him. It was lovely to see how much they admired him and appreciated his praise for all they did. They became like a family to us.

Soon after returning from Japan, he decided to write a book on how to learn the Japanese writing system. He renewed his relationship with Professor Edwin Reischauer who urged him to apply for an Ella Lyman Cabot Trust Grant, which he was awarded. He completed a book called *Scientific Kanji,* for which he did not obtain a publisher.

Vernon then began work on a new project, *The Love Rangers.* Vernon worked from 1977 to 1988 on creating seven self-published graphic novels of *The Love Rangers.* Drawing on his Army experiences, the series follows the lives and adventures of a number of officers, robots and members of a squad of genetically engineered Love Rangers (created to be only 3 feet tall) that live on the space ship called "Home." It is an immense structure, housing 35,000 individuals on its seven levels. While some of the action in the stories takes place on board, many of the episodes in his comic books take place on planets they visit.

The whole look and feel of this series was futuristic, even in 1977. The crew is racially mixed, and the ship is commanded by a male and female Shipmaster who share equally in all responsibilities. One of the dominant characters is Princess Tomi, who single-handedly leads her Mice People in their battle against the Owls for survival. There are robots and many futuristic devices used in the ship created by Vernon. According to Vernon, "Their mission and that of their great spaceship is to effect peaceful changes in critical situations through the use of Love." The fuel that powers the ship is feelings of discord and hate that emanate from different parts of the universe. At times the Love Rangers have to use weapons to control the warring inhabitants of the different planets they visit, but they attempt to first use their "love gas" to change the path of history. In the first book, the love gas helps change the consciousness of Count Ratalus from having a killing drive to flooding his mind with an understanding of history as well as nature's instinctive patterns. When this happens, a "well of human compassion overrides his coded savagery." He stops himself from killing Prince Tug, and they go off to work together peacefully for the betterment of the mice people and toward peaceful co-existence with their enemies, the Owls. Vernon sold these books primarily through the mail, and Harvard Square's comic book store, the Million Year Picnic.

Numerous writers and publications were intrigued with the stories and art of the series. A *Boston Phoenix* article in 1977 said, "There is another crucial difference between *The Love Rangers* and most other comic adventure series: there is no violence." Terry Beatty wrote in *The Buyer's Guide* in 1981: "The cross between Japanese cartooning and Basil Wolverton's science fiction work is charming. More importantly, Grant knows how to tell a story, and *The Love Rangers* is full of characters that seem much more real than any other more slickly drawn characters." Bhob Stewart, in a 1984 article in *The Comics Journal*, wrote, "...Grant, who has read numerous Japanese comics in the original Japanese... is at work on material that incorporates the Japanese sensibility on all levels of story, style, structure, page design and novelistic length... He continues to turn out his science-fictional tales of 'cosmic philosophy' that sometimes read as if Carl Barks lived in Tokyo." In 1985 Dale Luciano in *The Comics Journal writes*, "*Love Rangers* is a complex and intricately fashioned vision of life aboard a massive spaceship peopled by a race of 'masters' who have vowed to end all violence in nature and 'the urge toward savagery which has edged the long line of feeling beings since the beginning of time.' …A fanciful admixture of space opera and magical talking swords, a war between intelligent mice and owls, three-foot tall space cadets, and bizarre creatures called peckerworms… There is a pacifist theme, but there's an abundance of action that will satisfy adventure fans; and there are myriad imaginative touches."

One may wonder why a ten year veteran of the Army would develop this type of theme. Vernon always believed in the mission of the Army when he was a soldier and an officer, and continued all his life to support U.S. military actions over the years, until his passing in 2006. He believed strongly in supporting the United States, freedom and democracy. I had never known a professional soldier until I met him. And I learned from him that he, and many others in the military, could yearn for peace if it were at all possible, and work for it but still understand and accept the necessity of war.

After those many years of work on *Love Rangers,* Vernon developed a fascination with computers. In 1987, he began drawing many single panel cartoons, humorous scenes from our life in Cambridge, but also many poking fun at computers and their usage. We sold them as post cards through many book stores in the Cambridge and Boston area, as well as in the Computer Museum in Boston.

Vernon and I led a peaceful life together in Cambridge, Massachusetts, where we settled in 1973, got married in 1978, and lived together until Vernon's passing in 2006. It is a comfortable community for mixed couples. Both of our families accepted us, although it would have been hard for them to reject the notion of two people who were so happily and deeply in love being together. We were careful at times going into parts of Boston not to sit together on the train, knowing our relationship would not be welcomed by all. There was a time when we were running together past the generally liberal Boston College campus in Chestnut Hill area when a white man rolled down his car window and yelled the "N…" word at Vernon. We did go to the St. Patrick's Day parade in South

Boston in the early 1970s without incident. However, there were still a number of neighborhoods we avoided during the turbulent anti-busing movement of those times and after. It can be difficult to know who will accept or reject a relationship. One day as we waited for a bus close to our home, we sensed negative vibes from two young black women. Vernon told me later that they could not accept our love for each other but also would not have understood that he would have never married anyone who had not lived in Japan.

When I first met Vernon in Tokyo, he had been a runner for 15 years, running long before it was fashionable to do so. As I quickly realized he would be running daily, and knew I wanted to be with him, I realized I had better start running if I wanted to stay close to him. We lived in different areas of Tokyo and did not run together, but he gave me sage advice on how to start running. I had always wanted to be an athlete, so I welcomed his coaching and encouragement. He also impressed upon me that if we were living in Tokyo when the next Big One (a powerful earthquake) struck, it would be necessary to be healthy enough to run or at least walk back to our homes, as the subways would certainly not be working. So fear of earthquakes, desire to lose weight and to spend time with Vernon all conspired to make me into the serious runner I became with him.

Our first couple of years back in America we ran for fun and health. However, in 1976, I was bit by the Marathon bug. A woman from Wisconsin named Kim Merritt managed to win the Boston Marathon that April on a day it was 96 degrees. Somehow her victory made me feel I could run a marathon. We began our training for it and ran our first Boston Marathon in 1977. This began a period of 19 years, until 1996, that we ran the 26.2 mile distance together. We also became competitive in shorter distances, racing from 3.1 miles to 18.6 miles. Our competitors later told us since they did not like to see us at the starting line, knowing how we often placed in the top five of our age categories. Vernon often talked about how running would give him great ideas for his drawing. Our training runs also brought the enjoyment of the physical challenge, the scenery we passed by and each other's company.

A few years ago, I found the following story by Vernon on his thoughts on running.

"People often ask us, why do you run? Although we realize the politeness in many of the queries we do feel that the phenomenon of the act of running as a positive force in the lives of many moving animals is missed by a significant portion of the public at large. The idea of maximum physical effort as a goal and a positive influence on the overall health of the body is weighed down in some minds by the aggravation of breath and muscular stress coupled with the threat of collapse and prostration seem to point the mind away from any possible benefits. The possibility of the bodies' systems to move more efficiently for normal activities is a major plus. As with the auto which can run at 100 miles per hour, a 50 mile an hour pace is easily tolerated. Should public transportation be unavailable, the ability to run to a locations some 25 miles away in three hours is heartwarming as well as foot warming.

It is more difficult to explain just how exciting it is for us to view new or interesting sights together along the way and to discuss them as we move or later when we return home.

Running in the Boston area is very rewarding. There is so much to see. The widely disparate neighborhoods, the hilly sections, the marsh portions, the grand homes of Brookline and Newton, the long corridors of parkland and woods. Thankfully great tracts of the area in private and controlled trusts are not subject to ill-advised sub-divisions, the bane of many sections of the United States over the past ten years. Places such as Rockport and Gloucester have had some new building but have not been ruined by the rampant overbuilding going on at this time around Seattle. Anyone who might have thought that cemeteries and golf courses were a waste of space probably would have a change of mind if they witnessed the overbuilding of formerly pristine areas all over the nation. Many ecologists cite the need for natural habitat over undisturbed areas in order to sustain plant and animal life. Developers only seem to see land as something to build on… natural consequences be damned.

The character of the neighborhoods and areas in and around Boston change constantly with each quarter mile run… shaded to open to modern to historic to high rise to mansions to three-deckers to hilly to riverbank to oceanfront to garden choked to litter-strewn lots.

Running is built into the character of the region so the attitude of passersby for the most part is meritorious and positive. With so many runners, two more would usually not attract very much notice. However, being a dynamic duo we attract special notice. This is proved by the number of people who tell us they have seen us running in distant points or many who have seen us in their childhood and now in their mid-twenties. Other runner they forget almost immediately but they remember us… especially in our red knit hats in the winter time."

I also found another writing by him, about one of our early marathons.

Vernon Grant Personal Story of a Boston Marathon — first few miles of it

Weather breaks nicely in our favor, sunny and warm in the upper 50s to 60s. We wear light clothing and do not shiver our strength away waiting for the starting gun. Betsy wears her cheers eliciting white long sleeved shirt with the Red-White-Blue "WISCONSIN" emblazoned across the chest. I'm in an equally notable WIS-WISC-WISCO-WISCONSIN red t-shirt, a past present from Jean and Oliver Reese (Betsy's parents)

Betsy waits in line for the outdoor bathroom. We duck beneath the guide ropes and await the starting gun six or so minutes away. The gun goes off, the crowd roars, the runners clap and cheer the eight or so helicopters that clatter overhead. We are standing still yet. About a minute or so we inch forward. We cross the official starting line well over two minutes from the starting gun.

Step-step-carefully step. Make sure we don't trip on the person in front of us. A few tentative jogs forward are rewarded with abrupt stops as the running mass ahead of us picks up speed. Now we are 200 yards beyond the starting line and we are finally running— slowly, still mindful of the pressure of bodies all around. A stumble could be very serious.

At the half-mile point we begin to stretch our legs toward race pace. As we pass the clock for the first mile we read eleven minutes and twenty nine seconds. Many runners groan in shock. Most anticipated running the first mile in seven minutes and they are "behind schedule."

Betsy and I are pleased. We ran fourteen minutes last year so we are three minutes to the good. Betsy is really rolling now in that amazing aggressive running style I have seen so many times in the past. I wonder if she is running too fast. I go into my protective running crouch to save my thighs.

The air becomes thick and warmer. I am ecstatic. I love the heat and I can see it taking a toll on some nearby runners many of whom skip drinking at the early water tables. Tick-tick-tick we settle into a ground-covering steady stride that is well within the upper end of our practice preparations.

Note from Betsy – this was probably an early marathon by us, judging by the pace we ran.

Vernon's best marathon was Memorial Day in 1982, in the Maine Coast Marathon that started in Kennebunkport, Maine. He finished the race in 3 hours and 16 minutes at the age of 47. It was a very respectable pace as his average mile pace was 7 minutes and 31 seconds. He ran his last Boston Marathon in 1996 at the age of 61. It was his 33rd marathon. Afterwards, he said he had "retired" from it, happily came and watched me run by him on the course, and then met me at the finish line. But we continued to run together. On July 7th, 2006, we started out together, running over a Charles River bridge into Boston. I was setting out on a long run that day, and he parted with me there with his own plans to run back into Cambridge. Soon after I left, he had a heart attack. He was taken to a Boston hospital, in a coma from which he never emerged. He passed away peacefully on July 23rd.

He died doing what he loved. I located him by calling the police, after returning home much later from my run. He was not home and I knew he should have returned by that time. He had carried no ID on him, so the doctors guessed he was 46 years old. He was probably the "youngest" 71-year-old man they had ever seen. So he never grew "old."

Vernon was known in our Cambridge neighborhood for his smile, his happiness, his running and his kindness to children and adults. He was learned in many things, but was also a great listener. His skill as a Communications officer in the Army, his creations of the stories of *Point-Man Palmer* and cartoons in the military field as well as his science fiction world of *The Love Rangers* are his legacy.

As Vernon told the *Pacific Stars and Stripes* newspaper back in 1972, "Translating life into humor is the biggest thing with me." The following pages will prove he was true to his word. ✳

Vernon Grant:
ARTIST AND SOLDIER

Vernon Grant age 4.

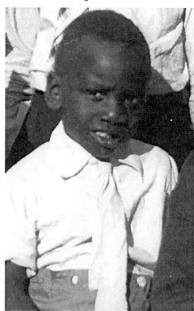

Vernon Grant High School Graduation 1952.

Vernon Grant Captain of Eagles Team 1951.

Travel to Thailand 1965.

VERNON GRANT

F.E.N. (FAR EAST NETWORK)
SOUTH CAMP DRAKE
ASAKA - MACHI
1964

BILL VERDEER
RADIO
FEATURE ANNOUNCER

1ST LT. VERNON GRANT
COMPTROLLER & CHIEF, U.S. ARMY ELEMEN
FAR EAST NETWORK
TOKYO, JAPAN

1st Lt. Grant Comptroller for Far East Network 1964.

Captain Grant 1966.

Captain Grant in Saigon Compound 1967.

Betsy and Vernon Grant Marriage Celebration 1978.

Vernon the Artist 1985.

Betsy and Vernon Grant 1995.

Vernon Grant finishing Wo-Zha-Wa Half Marathon 1985.

Maine Coast Marathon 1982 at mile 13.1 Vernon PR in 3 hours 16 minutes.

Vernon Grant:
ARTIST AND SOLDIER

Vernon Grant:
ARTIST AND SOLDIER

STAND BY ONE!
CARTOONS 1969

"... Call yer stupid mutt off me, goonfunkle!! ... I wuz only re-stacking yer louzy C-rations! ..."

"If that's a '*Hand*-shake Tour,' I'm Ho Chi Minh!"

"My wife says she doesn't want me to take an 'early out' for the Chicago Police."

"A c'mon now lieutenant . . . I know your last name is Bussy! . . . The 'P' was a typographical error."

"In case you're captured you can eat the message . . . I had it printed on rolled pizza! . . ."

"Say, Frank . . . You still got connections for penicillin shots? Miss Nyun gave me her regards."

VERNON GRANT

"Well, if it isn't the Army's answer to the Roto-Rooter man!"

"...You're a disgrace to the beret, Adams!..."

"...Frankly gentlemen, the V.C. in this area are getting *too* damned cocky!..."

"... My temperature's up!?!...Well now, what could have caused it to do a funny thing like that?!?..."

"Sure I've heard of 'Field Expedients' but this . . ."

"What do you mean you don't think this area is pacified?"

VERNON GRANT

"...Would you believe!!...
Bernie was actually *blown off*
his armored personnel carrier
three times in Vietnam!!..."
...isn't that *peachy*!!..."

VERNON GRANT

"...Iffin ya hold it up to the sun 'N' look real close ya can actually see *real beer* floating in between
the crud!..."

"I told you they weren't like the French!"

.."Yessir...all of the
essentials delivered by air"
. . .

"Goonfunkle . . . "You have my complete sympathy, I want out this MicKey Mouse outfit myself!"

Communique: MACV IO-Saigon— Many of the recaptured villages gave evidence of having undergone extensive indoctrination by Viet Cong counter - pacification teams.

"Whether it's combat or R & R, I always like to know
how people react in a pinch !"

"...GENIUS, SHEER GENIUS!..."

"...I THINK I'VE FOUND THE PERFECT SPOT TO SET UP OUR AMBUSH!..."

"... I'm anti-war, anti-draft, anti-fight ... Butcha might say I'm pro-living!
... So right *now* I'm anti-Viet Cong! ..."

ARTIST AND SOLDIER

"...I tell ya, Ken...it must be my good looks!...only five Saigon-teas and she can't keep her hands off me!..."

"...If they keep sneaking back to fight at this rate, we'll *never* make it back in time for' happy hour'..."

VERNON GRANT

"... Course, I'm no Inteligence Expert, but if I was you I'd rate this 'Current and Fairly Reliable!"

"... I know they're hiding in there. Colonel, the fumes from their *NUOC MAM* is turning the tree leaves red!
..."

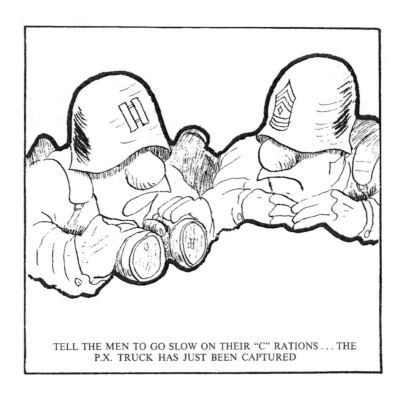

TELL THE MEN TO GO SLOW ON THEIR "C" RATIONS . . . THE
P.X. TRUCK HAS JUST BEEN CAPTURED

"Ssst . . . Hey G. I. . . . You want girl?"

"Well, *yes!* Miss Nancy Sweetwater, 889 Meridan Avenue, Tarzana, California! Say about suppertime?"

"... Say, Allen ... Grab yer canteen cup! ... My girl sent me a chocolate cake fer my birthday! ..."

"... I put two armored battalions on line, alerted division artillery, called for tactical air bombardments ... Including eight B-52 strikes, got ready for a fast heli-lift of the entire first and second brigades ... Then the 'enemy movement' turns out to be a march of the Bien Hoa *boy scout troop.*"

"Goonfunkle, you *Idiot*!
We *always* lose during
the first 20 minutes of
'Combat'!"

VERNON GRANT

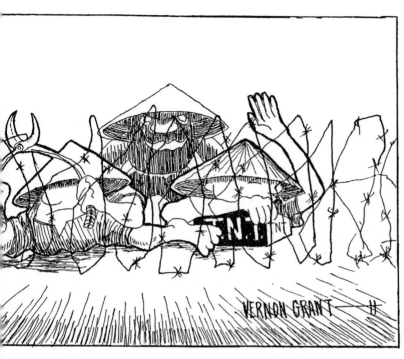

"...*NOW* WE'LL BLAST 'EM WHERE IT HURTS MOST!!..."

Vernon Grant:
ARTIST AND SOLDIER

POINT-MAN PALMER
AND HIS GIRLFRIEND
"INVISIBLE PEPPERMINT"
VIETNAM 1969

VERNON GRANT

... **PAULA PEPPERMINT,** DISPLAYING THE FORM WHICH GAINED HER A "**D**" IN CHEMISTRY HASTILY MIXES A BATCH OF SPECIAL FLUID IN HER BEDROOM LAB FOLLOWING A SPECIAL FORMULA FOUND IN AN OLD **USAFI** TEXTBOOK ∘∘∘∘ SHE —

— PREPARES THE SAME POWERFUL BREW MADE FOR **LASSIE** IN THE 1946 MOVIE "**INVISIBLE LASSIE VISITS GRANDMA FREKET'S HYDRANT FARM**" (NOT YET RELEASED) ∘∘∘∘

∘∘∘ AND —

THE EFFECTS ∘∘∘

... ARE FANTASTIC !!! ∘∘∘

∘∘YIPE!∘∘

SPROONG!

THE NEW PEPPERMINT! MINI- SKIRTED, INVISIBLE 40-22-36

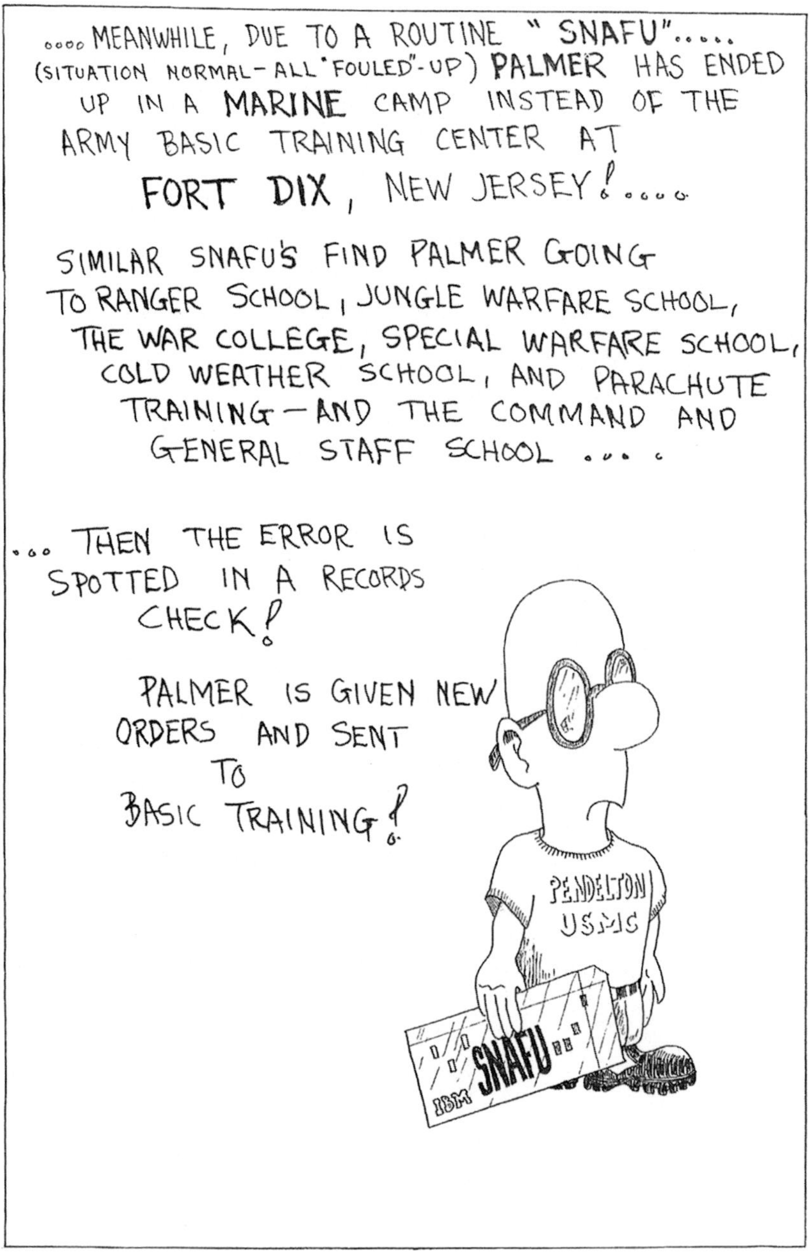

∘∘∘∘ MEANWHILE, DUE TO A ROUTINE " SNAFU".....
(SITUATION NORMAL—ALL "FOULED"-UP) **PALMER** HAS ENDED
UP IN A **MARINE** CAMP INSTEAD OF THE
ARMY BASIC TRAINING CENTER AT
FORT DIX, NEW JERSEY ! ....

SIMILAR SNAFU'S FIND PALMER GOING
TO RANGER SCHOOL, JUNGLE WARFARE SCHOOL,
THE WAR COLLEGE, SPECIAL WARFARE SCHOOL,
COLD WEATHER SCHOOL, AND PARACHUTE
TRAINING—AND THE COMMAND AND
GENERAL STAFF SCHOOL ....

... THEN THE ERROR IS
SPOTTED IN A RECORDS
CHECK !

PALMER IS GIVEN NEW
ORDERS AND SENT
TO
BASIC TRAINING !

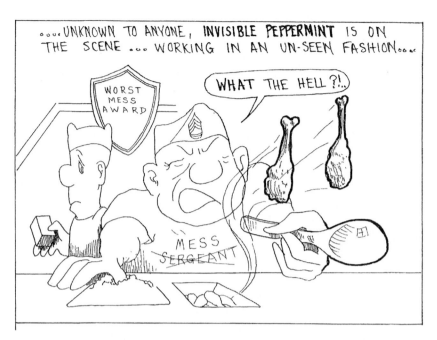

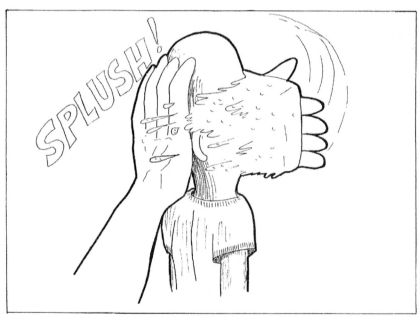

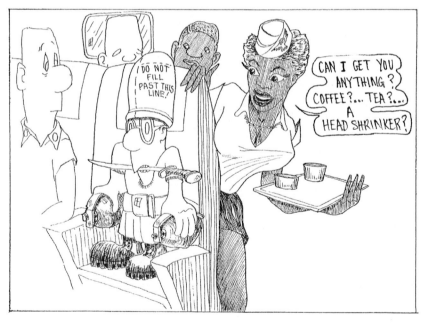

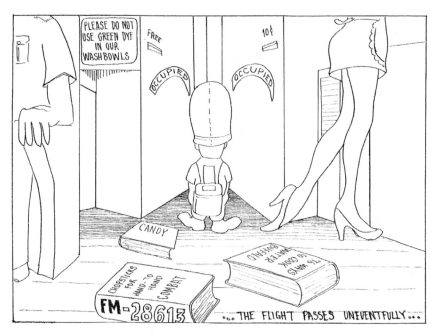

...THE FLIGHT PASSES UNEVENTFULLY...

...OTHERS MAY DWADDLE, BUT OUR HERO IS MADE OF STEELIER STUFF!...HE READIES HIS PRIME EQUIPMENT FOR COMBAT......

VERNON GRANT

VERNON GRANT

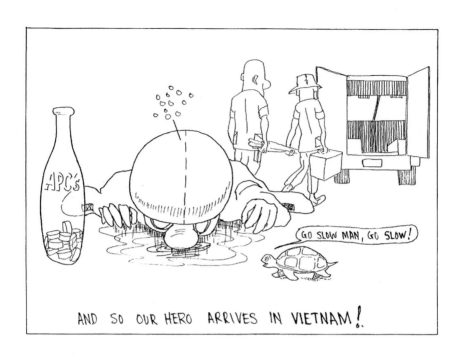

AMAZED BUT SATISFIED, THE BRASS GIVES PALMER THE AFTERNOON OFF TO SEE SOME OF THE SIGHTS IN **SAIGON!**....

... PALMER'S KEEN EYES (80-200) PICK UP A SUSPICIOUS MOVEMENT TO THE SIDE....

...A TERRORIST!...

TURNS AND COCKS A GRENADE- WEIGHTED ARM
AND DRAWS A BEAD
ON **PALMER'S**
SHINY DOME!...

...HE THROWS!...

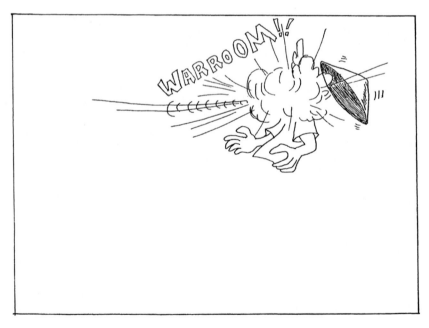

VERNON GRANT

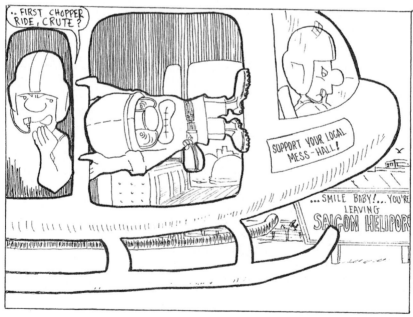

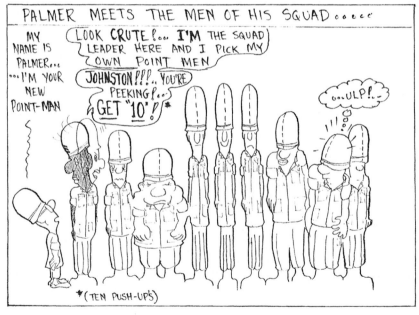

VERNON GRANT

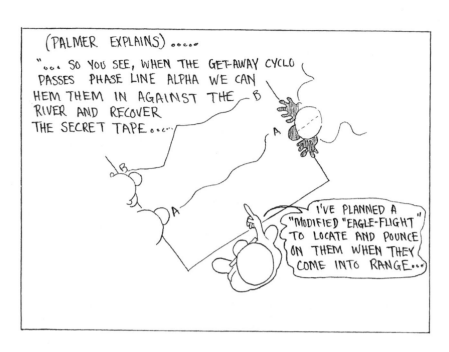

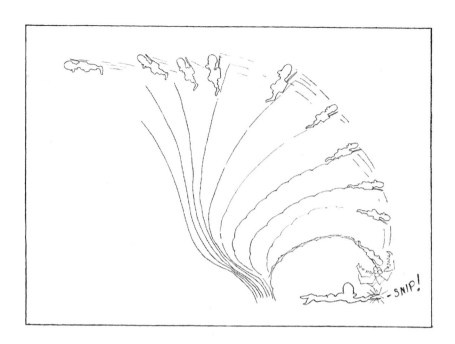

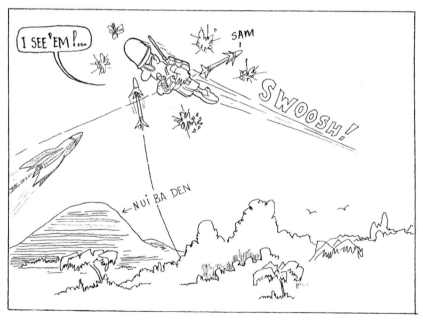

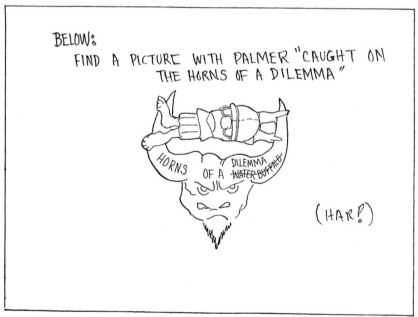

VERNON GRANT

DON'T MISS   BOOK TWO!
OF
POINT-MAN   PALMER

and read

ALL CHARACTERS, NAMES, AND
SITUATIONS ARE FICTICIOUS.

STAND BY ONE VERNON GRANT © 1969
CAMBRIDGE, MASSACHUSETTS.

Vernon Grant:
ARTIST AND SOLDIER

GLOSSARY, BIBLIOGRAPHY, ABOUT THE AUTHOR, VERNON'S RESUME

Glossary of Military Terms Used in Adventures of Point-Man Palmer in Vietnam

APC (Armored Personnel Carrier, which carried troops into the field of battle)

An **armored personnel carrier** (APC) is type of armored fighting vehicle (AFV) designed to transport infantry to the battlefield. APCs are colloquially referred to as 'battle taxis' or 'battle buses', among other things. Armored personnel carriers are distinguished from infantry fighting vehicles by the weaponry they carry (Wikipedia)

"Crute," which was short for recruit-The lowest ranked soldier in any branch of the military, usually one who has not yet completed basic training.

C-Rations: The C-Ration, or Type C ration, was an individual canned, pre-cooked, and prepared wet ration. It was intended to be issued to U.S. military land forces when fresh food (A-ration) or packaged unprepared food (B-ration) prepared in mess halls or field kitchens was impractical or not available, and when a survival ration (K-ration or D-ration) was insufficient. Development began in 1938 with the first rations being field tested in 1940 and wide-scale adoption following soon after. Operational conditions often caused the C-ration to be standardized for field issue regardless of environmental suitability or weight limitations. (Wikipedia)

E & E Evasion and Escape, as used in warfare (See class picture of Vernon Grant when in Officers' Training at Fort Benning, Ga.)

FM 22-5: This field manual provides guidance for Army wide uniformity in the conduct of drill and ceremonies.

G.I.: General Issue of the U.S. government, refers to a soldier.

Gold Flow Kit: first aid kit that held equipment that could test the severity of an injury to a soldier.

Latrine: Toilet, or simpler facility used as a toilet, usually without the toilet bowl, generally a pit in the ground.

MACV Regulation: Refers to a Military Assistance Command, Vietnam. Used in reference to MACV-SOG (Special Operations Group). MACV also was referred to as "Pentagon West" which was located at Than So Nut Air Base.

MPC (Military Payment Certificate): Military payment certificates, or MPC, was a form of currency used to pay U.S. military personnel in certain foreign countries. It was used in one area or another from a few months after the end of World War II until a few months after the end of U.S. participation in the Vietnam War – from 1946 until 1973. MPC utilized layers of line lithography to create colorful banknotes that could be produced cheaply. (Wikipedia)

Nuoc-mam: A Vietnamese food that was a fermented fish food product

OCS: Officer Candidate School

Point-Man: In modern military vocabulary, to take point, walk point, be on point, or be a point man means to assume the first and most exposed position in a combat military formation, that is, the leading soldier/unit advancing through hostile or unsecured territory. The term can be applied to infantry or mechanized columns. The soldier, vehicle, or unit on point is frequently the first to take hostile fire. The inherent risks of taking point create a need for constant and extreme operational alertness. However, ambushes often intend to let the point element past the prime killing zone in order to be maximally effective. Point position is often rotated periodically so as not to overtax the individual soldier/unit" (Wikipedia)

P.X.: Post Exchange, a general store in a military post that sells food as well as clothing and household items at discounts to the service people and their dependents.

Roger's Rangers: Rogers' Rangers were skilled woodsmen who fought for the British during the French and Indian War. They frequently undertook winter raids against French outposts, blended native-American techniques with pioneering skills and operated in terrain where traditional militias were ineffective. (Army News Service, June 5, 2014)

Robert Rogers, born in Methuen, Massachusetts, led the Rogers' Rangers, which were the precursor for the U.S. Army Rangers. Rogers' "Standing Orders" are still taught to U.S. Army Rangers.

Saigon Tea: A Kool-Aid flavored drink about the size of a shot glass drunk by Vietnamese women in the bars.

"Short": To be "short" for a soldier meant he or she was approaching the end of their term of service.

S.O.S.: reference to food served in the military, often means "shit on a shingle" and refers to a dish of creamed chipped beef served on bread.

Stand-by: To assume or maintain a position that is a state of readiness.

USAFI: United States Armed Forces Institute

USARV: US Army Reserve in Viet Nam

Viet Minh: The Army of South Vietnam

Vernon Grant Resume of 1975

Age 40
Born: 14 February 1935 in Boston, MA.
Address: 131 Putnam Ave. Cambridge, MA.
Five foot ten inches, Weight of 170 lbs.

SCHOOL
Houghton Grammar 1948
Rindge Technical High School 1952
Vesper George School of Art 1957
Sophia University, Tokyo, Japan, BA 1970
Sophia University, Tokyo, Japan, Graduate School to date

EMPLOYMENT
Houghton Mifflin Company 1956-1957
Military Voluntary January 1958
Basic Training—Fort Dix, New Jersey U.S. Army
Major Schools:
    Basic Army Administration Course
    Supply Sergeants Course
    Information Specialists School
    Officer Candidate School
    Basic Parachutists School
    Infantry Officers Communications Course
    Information Officers School
    Infantry Officers Associate Career Course

HISTORY
Commissioned a second lieutenant of Infantry 18 December 1961. Rose to grade of Captain. Discharged 7 January 1968 to begin university studies on 8 January 1968. Served tours of duty in France, Germany, Japan, Vietnam, Georgia, New Jersey, New York, and Colorado. In Japan, as the Chief, U.S. Army Element and Comptroller for the Far East Network February 1964 to June 1965. As Deputy Information Officer and Information Officer for the United States Army in June 1965 to June

1966. In Vietnam as Assistant Information Officer and Commanding Officer, 15th Public Information Detachment of the 25th Infantry Division December 1966 to January 1967. As Commanding Officer Signal Security Force-194th Military Police Company of the 1st Signal Brigade January 1967 to December 1967.

SPORTS
Running, Weight Lifting, Basketball, Baseball, Swimming. Captain of Intersettlement House All-Star Team (Phillips Brooks House) 1951. 165 pound Weight-lifting Champion, Cambridge YMCA 1956. Various Army awards for physical fitness.

WORK
Published books:
"POINT-MAN PALMER IN VIETNAM"
"POINT-MAN PALMER ON R&R IN TOKYO"
"STAND-BY ONE!"
"A MONSTER IS LOOSE IN TOKYO!"
Published Newspaper Cartoon Series
"A GRANT TIME IN JAPAN" Mainichi Daily News
"GRANT'S HEROES" Pacific Stars and Stripes
"GRANT'S GRUNTS" Pacific Stars and Stripes
"ACTION LINE" Mainichi Daily News

PRESENT ACTIVITIES
Co-Director in the formation of EAST/WEST Media. Completing a new instruction book on the Japanese writing system. Working on a book detailing the history and techniques of five major Japanese action cartoonists. Preparing two new cartoon series for U.S. syndication.

Bibliography

"*A Grant Time in Japan*" (published cartoon series-PCS) Mainichi Daily News 1969

"*Grant's Heroes*" (PCS) Pacific Stars and Stripes 1969

"*Grant's Grunts*" (PCS) Pacific Stars and Stripes 1969

"*Action Line*" (PCS) Mainichi Daily News 1969-1973

Stand-By One! 1969 a collection of single-panel Vietnam era cartoons Ad Interim Copyright Ai11695

Point-Man Palmer and His Girlfriend "Invisible Peppermint" 1969

Point-Man Palmer and His Girlfriend "Invisible Peppermint": Vietnam to Tokyo R&R 1970 Ad Interim Copyright Ai11696

A Monster is Loose in Tokyo! Tokyo, Japan and Rutland, Vermont: Charles E. Tuttle Company 1972

The Love Rangers 1, 1977

The Love Rangers 2, 1979

The Love Rangers 3, 1981

The Love Rangers 4, 1982

The Love Rangers 5, 1984

The Love Rangers 6, 1986

The Love Rangers 7, 1988

Ranger Readout, newsletter, 1987

The Comics Journal, #94, "*Samurai Superstrips*," 1984

Computer Cartoons Postcards (15) 1987

Author Profile for Betsy Reese Grant

Betsy Reese Grant grew up in the small friendly tourist town of Wisconsin Dells, Wisconsin. Her parents were Jean Dyer Reese and Oliver Reese Jr., and she had two sisters, Debbie and Lisa. She played trumpet and sang in chorus, was a Girl Scout, and canoed and hiked along the Wisconsin River. Betsy enrolled in classes at the University of Wisconsin-Madison in 1968. A judo class on campus taught by a Japanese businessman created the desire to spend a year studying in Japan. Meeting Vernon Grant in Tokyo at Sophia University in 1972 began a new chapter of her life.

In 1973, Betsy received a B.A. in History and she and Vernon returned to the U.S.A. by moving to Cambridge, Massachusetts, Vernon's home town. They were married in 1978. Vernon encouraged her to write, and in 1991, Betsy wrote the booklet about her great grandfather, *The Bennett Story – The Life and Work of Henry Hamilton Bennett*. Vernon taught her how to run, and they loved exploring new places on foot, and running in races together. Her new found fitness led to a career in selling health club memberships that Betsy pursued for twenty seven years. Travel became a major pastime for the Grants. Numerous trips to Wisconsin, trips to the Caribbean, to Barbados, and three trips on the Delta Queen steamboat on the Mississippi River brought Betsy and Vernon much happiness. After Vernon passed in 2006, Betsy stayed in the Cambridge area until 2011. She then moved back to Wisconsin Dells to be with her family.

Adventures of Point-Man Palmer in Vietnam was published in 2014. In 2015, Betsy had Vernon's book of single-panel cartoons, *STAND-BY ONE!* (1969) re-published. These two books have enabled Betsy to begin to fulfill her dreams of becoming a writer and exposing Vernon's work to new audiences. ✳

The World Learns about Vernon Grant

Since I published *Adventures of Point-Man Palmer in Vietnam* in November of 2014 and *STAND-BY ONE!* in October of 2015, I have engaged in much work to promote knowledge of Vernon Grant and what he created as an artist of military cartoons and science fiction. Numerous newspaper articles have appeared in the *Wisconsin State Journal, The Milwaukee Journal Sentinel, The Dells Events,* and the *Cambridge (Massachusetts) Chronicle.*

I have done 17 book signings and speeches at libraries and private group meetings.

I have been interviewed on two radio shows: The Callalloo Relationships Show of Cambridge Cable Television (Cambridge, MA); and "One Nation Under God" (Dallas, Texas). I have also had five television interviews: Callalloo Express Show (Cambridge, MA); February 16, 2015; Channel 3 (Madison, WI), May 1, 2015; Channel 27 (Madison, WI), November 6, 2015; Channel 15, (Madison, WI), July 14, 2016; and Channel 5 (Green Bay, WI), November 13, 2016.

In 2015, I joined the American Legion Auxiliary of Wisconsin Dells, WI and the Veterans of Foreign Wars Auxiliary of Reedsburg, WI to help our veterans. I have sold my books at conventions for both groups. As of the end of 2018, I have been a vendor at five, VFW state conventions in Wisconsin, Florida and Texas, and six American Legion Conventions in Wisconsin. I have also sold books at two National VFW Conventions in New Orleans, LA and Charlotte, NC and at The American Legion National Convention in Minneapolis, MN.

On July 28, 2016, I was honored to receive plaques from the city of Cambridge, MA and the Commonwealth of Massachusetts, stating that day as Vernon E. Grant Day.

Information about Vernon has appeared in the two books and three major magazine articles listed below in the past four years.

1. "Comic Book Creator" no. 8, Spring 2015, "The Art of Vernon Grant" (Discovering the "lost" graphic novelist, author of *Point-Man Palmer and Love Rangers*, Betsy Grant)

2. *The Comic Art of War. A Critical Study of Military, Cartoons, 1805-2014,* with a Guide to Artists. Christina M. Knopf, 2015, McFarland and Company, Inc., Jefferson, North Carolina.

3. *"Monster!"* Issue 22, October 2015, Editorializing! (Editorial by Tim Paxton) and "A Monster is Loose!–in Tokyo," Stephen Bissette (Part 1).

4. *"Monster!"* Issue 23, November 2015, Stephen Bissette, "A Monster is Loose!–in Tokyo" (Part 2).

5. *Encyclopedia of Black Comics,* Sheena C. Howard, 2017, Fulcrum Publishing.

My efforts are bearing fruit as Vernon E. Grant becomes better and better known as a major American cartoonist.

The End

VERNON GRANT